*BLUES & ROOTS / RUE & BLUETS*

INTRODUCTION BY

*Herbert Leibowitz*

*Jonathan Williams*

# BLUES & ROOTS
# RUE & BLUETS

*A Garland
for the Southern
Appalachians*

DUKE UNIVERSITY PRESS

© 1985 Jonathan Williams

Library of Congress Cataloging in Publication Data

Williams, Jonathan.
 Blues & roots, rue & bluets.

 1. Appalachian Region, Southern—Poetry.
I. Title.   II. Title: Blues and roots, rue and bluets.
PS3545.I52966B64  1985          811'.54        84–21126
ISBN 0–8223–0614–X
ISBN 0–8223–0615–8  (pbk.)
ISBN 0–8223–0636–0  (signed edition)

*"They Lord, Jonathan,*
*I want you to do hush!*
*I'm tickled to death"*

TUT BURNETTE
*Scaly Mountain, 1944*

*Introduction*

The poems of *Blues & Roots/Rue & Bluets* make up an unofficial oral history in verse of the Southern Appalachian folk often vilified and dismissed as hillbillies. Jonathan Williams' qualifications for "telling the lore" of these mountain folk are an unpatronizing affection for his unlettered and poor neighbors, a satirist's relish for collecting piquant samples of human folly, an acute ear for demotic speech, and an alert eye for found objects and graffiti. He weaves together the voices of these insular, opinionated people into a cultural fugue which reveals their ethos: their homespun oracles, racy apothegms, homeopathic nostrums for rheumatism and arthritis, their bluster and religious speculations. As chronicler, Williams knows when to duck out of sight and merely listen to the confiding talk and gossip (sometimes spiked with worm-wood) about weather, work, marriage, church, deathbed vigils, and local characters. The Iv Owenses and Daddy Bostains whittle or distill moonshine, rock or sit still, while unburdening themselves without a trace of self-consciousness. They may offer advice on planting:

> good time
> to plant corn
>
> when the hickory buds
> are as big
> as a squirrel's foot

or take aim, like the Hermit Cackleberry Brown, at human pretension and vanity:

> now some folks figure theyre
> bettern
>
> cowflop they
> aint
>
> not a bit
>
> just good to hold the world together
> like hooved up ground
>
> thats what

The vernacular words "cowflop" and "hooved up ground" bring the superior folks' airs to lumpy earth, the wry line breaks and white space between stanzas act out the moralist's virtuoso comic timing, while the final line, admitting no appeal from the hermit's judgment, snaps the poem and homily into place.

Like William Carlos Williams, Jonathan Williams believes that local speech can yield a rich mulch for poetry and render exactly the spirit of place: Three Mile Creek, Mount LeConte, iron chinquapin leaves, worts, spruce pines, and the people, always identified by name (Aunt Creasy, Uncle Jake Carpenter, Reverend Rufus A. Morgan), inflection, gesture, or tag (store-bought teeth, for example). With the lyrical precision of an amateur naturalist, one resident notices and discriminates details of color, scale, motion, and flavor ("Three Thefts from John Ehle's Prose" might easily be taken for a William Carlos Williams poem):

> every night
> the possums climb higher
> in the persimmon trees
>
> a red pumpkin
> in a row of yellow pumpkins
> in a field
>
> better'n
> a creek
>
> fulla syrup

Most of the Poems in *Blues & Roots / Rue & Bluets* are composed in a pungent dialect, as if Huck Finn had settled in the Blue Ridge or Smoky Mountains and continued to view the world's propensity for stupidity and meanness with the humorist's clear-eyed and trenchant truth-telling. Like Zora Neale Hurston in *Their Eyes Were Watching God* and Alice Walker in *The Color Purple*, Jonathan Williams spins his art out of the metaphoric sayings of the uneducated; their lives, messy and dignified, peevish and parochial (the redneck's bigotries are not sanitized; they are part of the record), take on a presence like the rhythms of a fiddler's tune, the wails of the blues, or the sassy proverbs and jests which the subliterate grammar and misspellings somehow enhance. Like the great eighteenth-century American Quaker botanist William Bartram, who hunted flowers in the Southern Appalachians, Jonathan Williams brings a zeal for accurate naming and a reverence for the poetry strewn abundantly in the fields, which he savors down to its succulent syllabic roots: "a flame azalea, mayapple, maple, thornapple/plantation/a white cloud in the eye of a white horse."

Just as Jonathan Williams' ear is attuned to the anthems of nature, so is his eye trained to spot a billboard by the side of the road that is the signpost of an unconscious cultural attitude. The following two examples have the wit and concision of a haiku:

U
NEED
JESUS
GOOD
BUDDY

O'NAN'S
AUTO
SERVICE

Jonathan Williams is not the amanuensis of these mountain folk or an ethnologist studying the mores of a clan; he is a sophisticated poet who can insert the lovely, mellifluous Latin name of the magnolia—*Liriodendron tulipifera*—among dialect poems, play off one of his incomparable long titles (a poem in its own right) against the epigrams the speaker in the poem instinctively shapes, and arrange typography into visual patterns and political commentary.

"If you despise a place long enough—this unruly continent, for instance—your own nature becomes despicable," Jonathan Williams muses in a letter. This mistake he never succumbs to. Etymologist, hiker, minstrel, ecologist, folklorist, and poet who excavates some of America's most unrespectable roots, he rescues a vanishing culture and enshrines it without sentimentality in the poems of *Blues & Roots/Rue & Bluets*. No literary critic with megaphone should have to proclaim the virtues of this wonderful, quirky, melodious book. The poems will linger in the reader's mind and on his tongue.

Herbert Leibowitz
*New York,*
*New York*
*May, 1984*

# A Note

An earlier version of this book was published by *Grossman Publishers*, New York (1971), with photographs by Nicholas Dean and typography by Dana Atchley. The author would like to thank Richard Grossman and Michael Loeb for permission to reprint a group of Atchley's realizations of the shaped poems.

Twelve texts have been pared; and thirty-three have been added—eight of which are printed for the first time. This much alteration made it impossible to conceive of using photographs. Nick Dean travels all the time from Maine; I travel a lot from Macon County, North Carolina, and our paths seldom cross these days. Also, it is our good fortune to have Jonathan Greene as designer on this occasion. His task has been to deal with a completely different sequencing of the poems.

For once the poet keeps his evangelical mouth shut and delivers no paraphernalia or apologies. He holds his piece. *Peace*—whichever. The only thing that needs to be said is that the range of the poems has spread a little on both sides of the Blue Ridge—as far as Pennville, Georgia to the west, and Rocky Mount, NC to the east. The folks are not very different.

*Blues & Roots / Rue & Bluets* was originally dedicated to Philip & Joan Hanes, of Winston-Salem, "for doing more than anyone we know to make North Carolina a place worth living in." There is absolutely no reason to change that sentiment, except to express sadness that Philip now must do his work alone. Do it, he will, from the strength of Joan's example.

JW
*Highlands,*
*North Carolina*
*November 21, 1983*

*BLUES & ROOTS / RUE & BLUETS*

*A Valediction For My Father, Ben Williams (1898–1974)*

all the old things
are gone now

and the people are
different

*Bea Hensley Hammers an Iron Chinquapin Leaf*
*On His Anvil Near Spruce Pine*
*& Cogitates on the Nature of Two Beauty Spots*

in the Linville Gorge I
know this place

now it's a rock wall
you look up
it's covered in punktatum all
the way to Heaven

that's a
sight

.

up on Smoky
you ease up at daybust
and see the first
light in the tops of the tulip trees

now boys that just naturally
grinds and polishes
the soul

makes it
normal
again

I mean it's really
pretty!

*The Hermit Cackleberry Brown, On Human Vanity:*

caint call your name
but your face is easy

come sit

now some folks figure theyre
bettern
cowflop they
aint

not a bit

just good to hold the world together
like hooved up ground

thats what

*Lee Ogle Ties a Broom & Ponders Cures for Arthuritis*

lands them fingers really
dreadfulled me I
couldnt tie
nary broom one

had to soak em in water
hot as birds blood

then I heard this ol man from Kentucky say
take a jug of apple juice just juice not cider
pour the epsum salts to it and
take as much as you kin

bein fleshy I kin take
right smart but
boys you know it moves a mans bowels
somethin terrible

well boys it just
naturally killed that arthuritis
lost me some weight too
and I
still tie thesehyar brooms

pretty good

## Old Man Sam Ward's History of the Gee-Haw Whimmy-Diddle

some folks say
the injuns made 'em
like lie-detectors
called 'em
hoo-doo sticks

feller
in Salisbury, Noth Caylini
made the first
whimmy-diddle I seen

I whittle seven
kind: thisuns king
size, thisuns jumbo, thisuns
extry large

here's a single, here's one
double, here's a triple and why right here
here's a forked 'un

been whittlin' whimmy-diddles come
ten year, I reckon you'd
care to see my other toys,
boys, I got some fine
flippers-dingers, fly-
killers and bull-roarers, I can

kill a big fly at 60 feet

watch here

*Paint Sign on a Rough Rock,*
*Yonside of Boone Side of Shady Valley*

BEPREPA
REDTO
MEETGO
D

*Daddy Bostain, the Moses of the Wing Community Moonshiners,*
*Laments from His Deathbed the Spiritual Estate*
*Of One of His Soul-Saving Neighbors:*

God bless her pore
little ol
dried up
soul!

jest make
good kindlin wood
fer Hell . . .

once we all grew shellot
potato onions everybody
around here have run out of
seed E. E. Seaton
of Jonesboro
Tennessee done heard
about this

.

the Fourth-a-July
Holiday
passed off in this part
very quiet

.

that snake were such
peculiar looking
to me I'm afraid I
couldn't give it justice
trying to describing it but it
didn't act mean like
it tryed to be
pretty like
it did

*Three Thefts from John Ehle's Prose*

every night
the possums climb higher
in the persimmon trees

.

a red pumpkin
in a row of yellow pumpkins
in a field

.

better'n
a creek
fulla syrup

.

*Three Graffiti in the Vicinity of*
*The Mikado Baptist Church,*
*Deep in Nacoochee Valley*

bulldogs
stamp out
dragon fire

.

# PEACHES HEAR

.

pleeze
vot fer lindin

*A Pileated Woodpecker's Response to Four Dogwood Berries*

kuk

kuk kuk

kuk·kuk

kukkuk

*A Blue Ridge Weather Prophet*
*Makes Twelve Stitches in Time*
*On the Twelfth Day of Christmas*

JANUARY

worst
winter

since
last!

FEBRUARY

if the catbirds chatter
winter's might nigh over

and spring is just around the corner but
we aint seen the corner yet

MARCH

sap-risin'
time
is lovin'
time,

o supine pine!

APRIL

this aint
Blackberry Winter

this is
Late Easter Squirt

MAY

good time
to plant corn

when the hickory buds
are as big
as a squirrel's foot

JUNE

when you tend
to your
own business
you got
a load,

come rain or come
shine

JULY

heavy
elder
bloom—

good
old time
sign

AUGUST

hit's frost
6 weeks from
when
the katydids
holler


SEPTEMBER

elder people said that gnat swarms
were a good sign of thunder storms

but since then,
only some light rain . . .


OCTOBER

heavy black
on the front end
of the woolly worm

bad weather
in the first go round
of winter time


NOVEMBER

first snow

get out,
wade in it
a little bit

old people, now dead,
said

## DECEMBER

if you would rather see mild weather
and see some sign that makes you sorter
think a little bit that it
is going to be a mild winter
it will make you at least for a little while feel
better about it—

before the real begins

*While Down at the Formicary, Time Flies*

inst
ant

COLD
BEER
TOGO

*Three Sayings from Highlands, North Carolina:*

but pretty though as
roses is
you can put up with
the thorns

*Doris Talley, Housewife & Gardener*

.

you live until you die—
if the limb don't fall

*Butler Jenkins, Caretaker*

.

your points is blue
and your timing's
a week off

*Sam Creswell, Auto Mechanic*

*Granny Donaldson Scoffs at Skeptics & the Uninitiated*
*As She Works Up a Cow-Blanket*
*(Of Homespun, Crocheting & Appliqué)*
*Up a Branch near Brasstown, Georgia*


Question:  whut fer
           thesehyar
           animules
           be,
           Granny?


Answer:  haint fer
         to name! why Adam's
         Off-Ox
         in thishyar
         Garden
         haint got
         no name
         neither
         yet


         but the Lord's
         liable to call
         thishyar
         tree
         Arber
         Vity


         hit's got
         thishyar
         sarpint
         in it

*A Blazon, Built*
*Of the Commonest of All Common Eurasian Weeds*
*Of the Fields and the Wayside*

```
O X E Y E
D A I S Y
C H R Y S
A N T H E
M U M L E
U C A N T
H E M U M
```

*The Ancient of Days*

would that I
had known Aunt Cumi
Woody

C-u-m-i, pronounced
Q-my

she lived in the Deyton Bend Section of Mitchell
County, North Carolina many years ago

there is one of Bayard Wootten's photographs of her
standing there with her store-bought
teeth, holding a coverlet

she sheared her sheep, spun
and dyed her yarn in vegetable dyes,
and wove the coverlet

in indigo, the brown from walnut roots,
red from madder, green from hickory ooze, first,
then into the indigo (the blue pot)

Cumi, from the Bible
(St. Mark 5:41)

Talitha Cumi:
*"Damsel, I say unto thee, arise!"*

she is gone, she
enjoyed her days

*Miss Lucy Morgan Shows Me a Photograph*
*Of Mrs. Mary Grindstaff Spinning Wool on the High Wheel*

Miss Lucy tells that one day
a visitor asked Mrs. Grindstaff
"What are you doing?"

she said "Spinning."

the tourist said
"Why doesn't it break?"

she said "Because I don't let it."

the charred heart does not break in Appalachia, they
have not let it . . .

the loom hums

there

*Aunt Dory Ellis, of Penland, Remembers*
*When She Fell in Her Garden at the Home Place*
*And Broke Her Hip in 19 and 56*

the sky was high,
white clouds passing
by, I lay
a hour in that petunia patch

hollered,
and knew I was out of whack

*Mrs. Sadie Grindstaff, Weaver & Factotum,*
*Explains the Work-Principle to the Modern World*

I figured
anything anybody
could do a lot of I
could do a little
of

mebby

*Aunt Creasy, On Work:*

shucks
I make the livin

uncle
just makes the livin
worthwhile

*Uncle Iv Surveys His Domain from His Rocker*
*Of a Sunday Afternoon as Aunt Dory Starts*
*To Chop the Kindling*


Mister Williams
lets youn me move
tother side the house

the woman
choppin woods
mite nigh the awkerdist thing
I seen

*The September Satisfaction of Uncle Iv Owens:*

I got
a rat-proof
crib!

*Three Bears of Different Sizes,*
*Dreaming from Three Hollow Logs*
*On Mt. Kephart in the Great Smokies*
*On a Warm Day in February*

*The Colossal Maw from War-Woman Dell, Georgia*

more mouth on
that woman

than ass
on a goose

ASS is NICE

best thing
for roomatiz,
Homer, is

a great big ol messa
Woolly-Booger

if God
made anything better
he kep it
for Hissef

but boys lemme
tell you:

DON'T EAT NO
HAIRPIE
ON FRIDAY!

*John Chapman Pulls off the Highway towards Kentucky*
*And Casts a Cold Eye on the Most Astonishing Sign*
*In Recent American Letters*

# O'NAN'S AUTO SERVICE

*Stone Sign*
*By the Temple Congregational Community Church's*
*Resident Theologaster*
*On the Banks of the Tallulah River*

U
NEED
JESUS
GOOD
BUDDY

*Logger to Dozer*

if you work
for me,
son,
you got to
shit
and go
get
it

*Cracker-Barrel Reveries on the Tune "Pax Americana"*

*"Us common people run this country!"*   GEORGE WALLACE


feller over in
franklin
says hes got thishere book
says that fbi feller hoover
says that nigger preacher kings
nothin
but a tarnation communist

and i reckon you boys
heared on the tv this
walter jenkins hes
some kind of unnatchrul sex prevert why
you know them seven chillun
must be lightbulbs
you just know it

just like you know ol castro
and them jew boys in new york
got us into veetnam

some things be's plain obvious

why the barber feller was sayin
just yesterday
he said put the bombs to em boys drop em
all over them russkis and
the dadblame chinamens too and
might as well drop em on ol dee gawl
too hes got the big mouth dont he

i mean put it to em all
i mean buddy we could stop all this foolishness up north

why some things be's plain obvious

*people get*
*what they want*

*A Mnemonic Wallpaper Pattern for Southern Two-Seaters*

*A Ride in a Blue Chevy from Alum Cave Trail to Newfound Gap*

goin' hikin'?
git in!

o the Smokies are ok but me
I go for Theosophy,
higher things, Hindu-type philosophy,
none of this licker and sex, I
like it
on what we call the astral plane,
I reckon I get more i-thridral
by the hour

buddy, you won't believe this but
how old you reckon the earth is?
the earth is
precisely 156 trillion years old—
I got this book from headquarters in
Wheaton, Illinois
says it is!

I'll tell you somethin' else:
there are exactly 144 kinds of people on this earth—
12 signs and the signs change
every two hours,
that's 144, I'm Scorpio,
with Mars over the water

here's somethin' else innerestin':
back 18 million years
people was only one sex, one sex only . . .
I'd like to explain that,
it's right here in this pamphlet,
50 cents . . .

never married, lived with my mother in Ohio,
she died, I'm over in Oak Ridge
in a machine shop, say,
what kind of place
is Denver?
think I'll sell this car, go to Denver,
set up a Center . . .

name's Davis,
what's yours?

*Dear Reverend Carl C. McIntire:*


Just a note
to let you know
we are listening to you
on Station
K-I-K-E
in Richmond,
Virginia

There are four of us Fundamentalist Baptist ladies
who ride together at 7:30
to the shirt factory and the napalm plant
and we always listen to your
"20th CENTURY REFORMATION HOUR"
every day
after the early morning
"MO-TOWN-SOUND-SHOW" with
"Urethra & the Catheters"—

you both groove, baby,
I mean you let it *all* hang out
and no doubt!

So when you laid that wicked-world bit
on our heads Friday we felt we should be prepared
to meet God and goodness we sure would feel lost
without your spiritual uplift in our new pink
Dodge Polara . . .

Yours agin sin and keep keepin' those darkies
from a destroying *our* freedom,
zang-a-dang!

Myrtle-Jean Pugh, Co-Captain
James River Industrial League of
White Women Bowlers,
Team #16

*Who Is Little Enis?*


Little Enis is
"one hunnert an' 8olbs of
dynamite
with a 9-inch
fuse"

his real name is
Carlos Toadvine
which his wife Irma Jean
pronounces *Carlus*

Carlos says
*Toadaveenie* is a eyetalyun name,
used to be lots of 'em
round these parts

Ed McClanahan is the World's Leading Little Enis Freak
and all this information comes to you from a weekend in Winston
with Big Ed telling the lore of Lexington, Kentucky,
which is where Enis has been hanging it out for years and years,
at Boots Bar and Giuseppe's Villa and, now, The Embers,
pickin' and singin' rockabilly style

Carlus ain't what he was
according to Irma Jean's accounts
(and even to his own):

he was sittin' there one night in the kitchen at home
tellin' stories and talkin' trash about Irma Jean—
with her right there with her hair put up in them pink plastic curlers—
about how these days how he likes to pop it to her dog-style
just now and again and how she likes it pretty damn well
when they wander all over the house

and end up in the living room corner—
"I'm just afraid Carlus will run us out the door and down the street
opposite the automatic laundry . . ."


The 9-inch fuse hung down Enis' left leg
is called, familiarly,
Ol' Blue

Ol' Blue used to be in the pink!—
way in . . .

Blue has a head on him like a tom-cat
and ribs like a hongry hound

and he used to get so hard
a cat
couldn't
scratch it . . .

but now that Enis has the cirrhosis
and takes all thesehere harmones
Ol' Blue just don't
stand up
like a little man
and cut the mustard
anymore

but Enis will smile and say
let's all have a drink, maybe I can drown thatthere liver of ours,
it's no bigger'n a dime nohow anymore, it just floats in there . . .

Hey, Blue, let's shake that thang!
Turn a-loose this oldie
by my boy Elvis—
a golden oldie!
let's go, Blue!

And off they go
into the Wild Blue
Yonder in the Blue
Grass . . .

Carlos & Blue,
thinking of you . . .

*Hail & Farewell!*

*Plain, Absolutely Unrefined*

yessir buddy
three moon pies and a nehi
grape

you see them five boys
on that fence across the street
hangin out actin cute

reckon i could fuck
every last mothers son in
just one week

if i was lucky
and had me maybe just one more
moon pie

I. SENATORIAL

the Stem of Jesse's Rod
does not change its underwear
East of Eden

Underwear changes
it

2. DEMANDING SIGNPOST, NEAR SEAGROVE, ON THE WAY TO JUGTOWN:

# ERECT 8

3. RED PIG BARBECUE #2, CONCORD

Irene:
Whuddya git fer Christmas, Bernice?

Bernice:
Everything I wanted: a rifle and a blender!

4. COLONEL BURRUSS DROPS A LINE

digg'n holes,
　　　　　fix'n fences,
　　　　　　　　　eat'n ham meat . . .

5. CHAPEL HILL

"Tom's dick's
harder'n times
in '29"

6. THE ANTHROPOPHAGITES GET DOWN
ON A BARBECUE SIGN ON
HIGHWAY NC 107 SOUTH OF HAMLET

# EAT
# 300 FEET

7. ROLLING INTO NASH COUNTY, AM-RADIO REVEALS THAT

Ravishin' Ruby

sleeps in a
bunk in the back . . .

she's poured
a lotta coffee

in her time

Ravishin' Ruby,

glued to the tube,
never saw brown fire
coming up the highway

or her simple heart
cut out at K-Mart

8. A NEW NUNC DIMITTIS!
   TSM (1917–1982)

dawgone it
dad gum it
dad rat it

MONK DE
FUNK

*Three Ripples in the Tuckaseigee River*

# tsi ksi tsi
# ksi tsi ksi
# tsi ksi tsi

*A Week from the Big Pigeon*
*To the Little Tennessee River*

I.  DAVENPORT GAP

the tulip poplar is not a
poplar it is a magnolia:
*Liriodendron tulipifera*

the young grove on the eastern slopes of
Mt. Cammerer reminds me
of the two huge trees
at Monticello, favorites
of Mr. Jefferson;

and of the Virginia lady
quoting Mr. Kennedy:

the recent gathering of
Nobel Prize Winners at the
White House—the most
brilliant assemblage
in the dining room
since Mr. Jefferson
dined there

alone . . .

*a liriodendron*
*wind, a liriodendron*
*mind*

## 2. TRI-CORNER KNOB

here the shelter's
in a stand of
red spruce and balsam fir

for dinner: lamb's-quarters,
cress from the streams
on Mt. Guyot,
wood sorrel, and
cold Argentine beef, chased with
tangerine kool-aid

## 3. COSBY KNOB

DeWitt Clinton (besides
looking like Lon
Chaney on tobacco-tax stamps)
comes to the eye
in *Clintonia borealis*—

of which fair green lily
there are millions
on this mountain

it is a mantle
for fire-cherry, yellow birch,
and silver bell

## 4. FALSE GAP

no *Schwarzwald* stuff,
*keine Waldeinsamkeit,*

no magic grouse, no
Brothers Grimm—just

Canadian hemlock, mossed and lichened,
like unto maybe
Tertiary time . . .


too much for a haiku?
you hike it and see


5. LECONTE HIGH-TOP

under the rondelay
the sun

into the wind and rain a
winter wren

again, again—

its song
needling the pines


6. SILERS BALD

just in front of the
round iron john
in the beech grove

the fresh bear droppings
give you

something
to think about

*What Are the Names*
*Of the More Remote Mountains of Northwestern Georgia?*

Horseleg

John                    Dug Down

Horn

Little Sand

Lavender

Dirtseller

Turkey

*The Traditionally Accommodating Spirit of the Mountains*
*Shows Up in Neon in Franklin, NC,*
*Once Nikwasi, a Cherokee Capital*

*cafe*

*Selected Listings from the Western Carolina*
*Telephone Company's Directory (Bryson City, Cashiers,*
*Cherokee-Whittier, Cullowhee, Franklin, Highlands, Sylva)*

| | |
|---|---|
| Applewhite Max | Moss Floda |
| Bell Corydon | Norton Paschal |
| Chiltoshey Going Back Mrs | Orr Deaver |
| Cody Verlous | Owl Frell |
| Cope Ode | Painter Fern |
| Cox Plato | Peek Benlon |
| Crisp Gentry | Polk James K |
| Dalton Dock | Pickens Excellent Fine |
| Evitt Delphia Mrs | Picklesimer Turley |
| Flack Kolin | Queen Kennith |
| Foxx Zollie Rev | Quiet Lily |
| Game Gertrude | Rogers Gas Island |
| Gibson Pink | Rainwater Veezey |
| Good Colon L Rev | Strong Hope |
| Gribble Geneva | Sneed Cam |
| Huggins Rass | Shook Troy |
| Imperato Pat | Tweed Strang |
| Jones Vestal | Undergrowth Homer |
| Johnson John Bunion | Van Lyon |
| King Hill | Webb Zero |
| Keener Maiden | Wold Maude |
| Kiser Julian (Bug) | Womack Kibby |
| Keen Yeoman | Whittle Chester |
| Love Jeter | Ward Milas |
| Mashburn Angeline | Wood Cooter |
| Muse O.U. | Youngbird Rufus |

o
n
e
cO On
o
o
n
o
n
e
l
o
n
e
p
i
n
e

*Aubade*

you could hear an ant
fart
it was that
quiet

*Jeff Brooks, Wagon-Master of Andrews,*
*En Route to Franklin through the Nantahalas:*

no
other
sound

except

the creak
of leather

*What Are the Names*
*Of the Three Tutelary Hamadryads*
*Of the Hickory Grove*
*On Dirty John Creek in the Nantahalas?*

BUSTHAID

BLOCKADE

POPSKULL

*A Chorale\* of Cherokee Night Music*
*As Heard through an Open Window*
*In Summer Long Ago*

WAHUHU WAHUHU WAH
UKU UGUKU UGUKU UGU
U HUHU HUHU HUHU HU
LU LALU LALU LALU LA
TU TALATU TALATU TAL
LILI TSIKI LILI TSIKI LILI
IKIKI TSIKIKI TSIKIKI T
U KAGU KAGU KAGU KA
WAYA WAYA WAYA WAYA
YEAH YEAH YEAH YEAH
NA GUNA GUNA GUNA GU
SASA SASA SASA SASA S
UNU KUNUNU KUNUNU
DUSTU DUSTU DUSTU D

\* screech owl / hoot owl / yellow-breasted chat / jar-fly / cricket / carolina chickadee / katydid / crow /
wolf / Beatles/ turkey / goose / bullfrog / spring frog

*Night Landscape in Nelson County, Kentucky*

ah, Moon, shine
thou as amber in thy
charred-keg, hickory sky . . .

still as a still, steep
as a horse's face

*The Custodian of a Field of Whiskey Bushes*
*By the Nolichucky River Speaks:*


took me a pecka real ripe tomaters up
into the Grassy Gap
one night

and two quarts of good stockade
and just laid there


sippin and tastin and lookin agin the moon
at them sorta fish eyes in the jar
you get when its right


boys Im talkin about somethin
good

*Standing by His Trailer-Studio*
*In Campton, Kentucky,*
*Edgar Tolson*
*Whittles a Few Syllables*



that piece
thats what some folks call a *spinach*
or some damn thing

i got it
offn a match box

it needs wings
and a lions tail


some damn woman down in Lexington
wants it

O


GL  RY

*A Rhyme Without End for Howard Finster*
*About How It All Began in the Country Near Lookout*

I thought at first of swarms of bees ...
But, sure enough, it was God Who was shooting the breeze,
looking about in thishere grove of red trees,
Who said to Howard (down there on his knees),
"Howard, your warm arm, please,
what we need down here is a man who 'sees'
the glory stored in *breeze* and *trees*
and what art there is in words to bring folks ease."

Swarm for the Lord like bees!
Sing like honey on its knees!

# The Lord, Working in Mysterious Ways, at Scaly Mountain

married a Dryman and
her sister got married to Hays Bryson
you probably remember Hays

what's happened to Hays
I used to like old Hays

Hays and his mrs they's
chief cook and bottle washer
down at the Dillard House

Hays' youngest boy Larry
had a lump grow up on his wrist
they cut it open
sent a specimen to Florida
you know it was that galloping bone cancer
had to take a piece out that long
and naturally you have to wonder about it

you know it seems like Hays
has had more than his fair share of trouble
some folks say that life's dumber than a two-dollar dog
and I believe it

what became of his boy Forrest
who had the rheumatic fever
I used to like Forrest
used to give him books
when he was laid up in bed
and couldn't get out

Forrest well lord why he almost got plumb killed
when that car ran over him
two or three years back
he can do light work but he'll
never be right

Forrest must have been about 17
when I last saw him
he'd had an operation
gotten strong
he was pitchin' hay into
Uncle Iv Owens' barn
sweat pouring off his back
he had those fine blue eyes

and now maybe he's 37
sittin' around a house in Mountain City Georgia
thinkin' about his brother's arm . . .

## Cobwebbery

the best spiders for soup
are the ones under
stones——

ask the man who is one:
plain white american

(not blue gentian red indian yellow sun black caribbean)

hard heart, cold
mind's found

a home
in the ground

"a rolling stone, *nolens volens*,
ladles no soup"

maw, rip them boards off
the side the house

and put the soup pot on

and plant us some petunias
in the carcass of the Chevrolet

and let's stay here
and rot in the fields

and sit still

*The Autochthon*

if it was Clinch Valley, Virginia
you'd figure:
James Stephens
was a Meulungeon,

some kin to the famous Morning Glory Finch,
half-Indian / half-Raleigh's Eden,
gone back to
ground . . .

but this is Newton County,
Arkansas Ozarks—
place with overhill towns
named Parthenon, Ben Hur, Red Star,
Yellville, Verona, Snowball . . .

James Stephens lives in the woods:
one billy goat, two dogs, assorted ants,
one black cat

he plays the concertina for them
late at night
in women's clothes . . .

"You Are My Sunshine"—
*contra natura*

he often misses his dinner
that they may eat

"You Are My Sunshine"—
*contra natura*


.

on the table,
along with these photographs by Cherel Winett,
is an epigram
by Edward Dahlberg:

"I abhor the cult of the same that is the universal malady today,
and acknowledge I'm different, since I came into the world
like the four elements:
emotion, strife, remorse and chagrin."


I'd like to see James Stephens take a picture of Richard Nixon,
or Richard Avedon, from back in there where those eyes of his are—
a place with topsoil in the character


the face
looks like J. Paul Getty
without a dime,
with character


the last face I saw anywhere near its equal,
that was Clarence Schmidt's, he
was sitting in the derelict car in the Wonder-Garden
on the Ohayo Ridge near Woodstock:


"Call me Clarence, boys!
you from some sort of foundation?
—no, no use writing a poem,
NBC's already did it, screened it all over California . . .
bad thing too, these hippies come,
steal me blind . . .
yes, well, help yourselves, I got to fix thishere foil icicle
tree, see . . ."

like Ol' Man Turley Pickelseimer,
who hid out from the guvmint during some war
in a cave down in Blue Valley
which became known as 'Pickelseimer's Rock House,'
I hope James Stephens stays hid,
plays his goat-songs,
stays off tv and out of Fort Smith


.


as you know, Stephen Sykes,
of Aberdeen, Mississippi,
made the mistake of going into Memphis one night and later remarked

"Don't talk so much.
Keep your mouth
closed
and your bowels
open,

and believe in
Jesus!"

*Osiris, from His Cave to Spring:*

for the Scripture is written:
"Plants at One End, Birds at the Other!"

houseleek & garlic,
hyssop & mouse;

hawk & hepatica,
hyacinth, finch!

crawl, all
exits

from
*hibernaculum!*

*Ye Rattle-Snake*




of the thickness / of the Small / of a lusty Man's Leg . . . . . . . . . .

*A Votre Santé*
*At The Headwaters of the Santee*

"which water we drank of, it
coloring the excrements of Travelers,
by its Chalybid Quality,
as black as a Coal"

(*John Lawson*)

*The Chiromantic Philologist; or,*
*A Brief Word from Charles Olson:*


*cave*, it means cave

CHOLUK     (Choctaw jargon per Mobilian Trade Language,
                 Gulf Coast and Southeast, 1539 and pre-)

CHALAQUE (Portuguese, Gent. of Elvas' De Soto Chronicle,
                 1557)

CHERAQUI (French, Penicaut, 1699, in contact with Lower
                 Dialect, where *l* becomes *r*)

CHEROKEE (Eng. Gov. Johnson, 1708, probable ancestor of
                 P. Johnson, Gov. of Miss., still talking
                 Choctaw jargon)

the Cherokee form is *Tsalagi*, and means nothing;
they call themselves *Yunwiya*,
the principal people

*A Note\* on the European Background of
Sempervivum Tectorum, Which We Now Call
'Houseleek' or 'Hen-and-Chickens'*

this wort,
which is named *prick madame*,
is produced on walls, and in stony places,
and on downs,
and on old barrows,

and from one root
it sendeth forth many minute boughs,
and they be full of leaves,
minute and long,
and sharp and fat,
and well oozy,
or *succulent*,

and the root of this wort
is without use!

\* from the Rev. Thomas Oswald Cockayne's
  *Leechdoms, Wortcunning & Starcraft of Early Eangland*

*A Round of Nouns in Jackson County*

Rough Butt Creek
*to*
Bearwallow Fork
*to*
Snaggy Bald
*to*
Mayapple Gap
*to*
Fern Mountain
*to*
Soapstone Gap
*to*
Rocky Face Cliff
*to*
Alum Knob
*to*
John Brown Branch
*to*
Hornyhead Mountain
*to*
Niggerskull Mountain
*to*
Sugar Creek Gap
*to*
Rough Butt Creek

*The Action During the Pour-Down\**
*At Plum Orchard Gap Shelter,*
*September 29, 1964:*

*6:15 a.m.*
one Samson's Snakeroot in a clump of Galax
at the spring

*10:23 a.m.*
sluggish black salamander grabs bristling cricket
by left hind leg
but      lets            go

*12:50 p.m.*
fresh deer droppings on the Trail
full of orange persimmon seeds

*2:47 p.m.*
a ripe persimmon plops on the ground
among the dogwoods

*4:20 p.m.*
one pink plastic rat-tail comb
washed clean in the fireplace

*5:06 p.m.*
a red spider rides, a yellow maple leaf
glides to earth

*8:31 p.m.*
flashlight batteries fade out
reading Joseph Mitchell's profile
of Little Joe Gould

\* at Rosman, on the North Fork of the French Broad River below the Balsam
Mountains, the rain is reportedly 16 inches in less than 24 hours

*Mr. Rufus Cook*
*Blairsville, Georgia*

Dear Mr. Cook,
The past few weeks I have been attempting to locate some Indian rock carvings which my reading tells me are in Union County. These carvings do not seem to be those at Track Rock Gap. I have been there three or four times and the position and surroundings do not agree with what is in the books. When I talked to some men working on the new highway up to Jack's Gap, one of them said you would know if anybody did. So said the look-out ranger up on Brasstown Bald. I am interested because I am a writer and photographer, and because the Southern Highlands is the part of the world I like best. I've hiked the Appalachian Trail from Georgia to New Hampshire, and I've been exploring around Highlands since 1941, so, I know a little—but not nearly enough.

The first reference I encountered was a paper, "On the Pictographs of the North American Indians," by Garrick Mallery. This is contained in the *Fourth Annual Report of the Bureau of Ethnology*, published in Washington, DC in 1886. On page 23 it says this:

"Dr. M. F. Stephenson mentions, in *Geology and Mineralogy of Georgia* (Atlanta, 1871, page 199), sculptures of human feet, various animals, bear tracks, etc., in Enchanted Mountain, Union County, Georgia. The whole number of etchings is reported as one hundred and forty-six."

The only other mention is of an incised boulder in Forsyth County, Georgia, first noted by Charles C. Jones, Jr., in *Antiquities of the Southern Indians, etc.* (New York, 1873, page 377). . . . It seems a little odd that there is no mention of Track Rock.

Next I came across a legend of Enchanted Mountain in *Georgia's Landmarks, Memorials, and Legends* (Atlanta, 1913, 2 volumes, pages 457–60 in volume two), by Lucian Lamar Knight. This work strikes me as much less reliable than the Government publication mentioned initially above. However, it has a much fuller description. Mr. Knight indicates that his information comes from an old scrap-book belonging to a Dr. Stevenson, of Dahlonega. (The name leads me to wonder whether or not Dr. Stevenson is not the Dr. M. F. Stephenson of the first reference?)

Let me quote parts of this account, and see what you make of it:

"Ten miles north of the Blue Ridge Chain, of which it forms a spur, is the Enchanted Mountain, so called from the great number of tracks and impressions of the feet and hands of various animals to be found in the rocks. . . . The number of well-defined tracks is one hundred and thirty-six, some of them quite natural and perfect, others rather rude imitations, and all of them, from the effects of time, have become more or less obliterated."

He notes 26 impressions of human feet. "A finely-turned hand, rather delicate, may be traced in the rocks near the foot of the great warrior." He mentions horse tracks, turkeys, turtles, terrapins, a bear's paw, a snake, and two deer.

As to the location he says: "On the morning of the 3rd of September, 1834, our party left the Nacoochee Valley. . . . At six o'clock we arrived at the summit of the mountain. . . . We advanced to the foot of the rock and spread out our breakfast on the 'table of stone.' . . . Around us were piled huge heaps of loose rock. . . . The rock upon which these impressions were found is an imperfect sort of soapstone. . . . After excessive fatigue and no little danger, we were now ready to return home, but before descending the long slope we paused to feast our enraptured eyes upon one of the most magnificent panoramas to be found on the North American continent. . . . On the east is Tray, peering above the clouds . . . while southward, in the distance, is the majestic figure of Old Yonah."

If one takes a Geodetic Survey map and tries to take into consideration all these facts, it becomes *very* confusing. But, Track Rock is unlikely (1) it is not a spur of the Blue Ridge; (2) its elevation is very low and certainly not on a top; (3) Tray is not east from there, but southeast; (4) even in 1834 when men had good legs it's doubtful that one would walk there from Nacoochee Valley—definitely not by 6 a.m.; (5) the carvings—those that are left after the vandals—do not fit the description and the number.

I talked to a Mr. Elrod in Robertstown. He'd never heard of anything like Enchanted Mountain. His son, Hugh Elrod, a policeman in Cleveland, hadn't either, but he sent me to Mr. Charlie Winn in Choestoe Valley. No luck there either. Several mountains were mentioned with rocks or cliffs on them (Blood, Cowrock, Naked Mountain, and Steedy Mountain)—but not carvings that anyone knew. So, either the books are talking about Track Rock Gap in completely inaccurate terms, or else some exceptional carvings have been lost and forgotten.

If you have any information, I would certainly appreciate very much hearing from you. I am sending a copy of this letter to the Department of Archaeology at the University in Athens, in the hope that someone there has access to further references than my own library affords. Thank you very much for troubling to read all this. Perhaps we can help find a very mysterious mountain?

*Jonathan Williams*

*The Laconic, Contrapuntal Nocturne of Two Goatsuckers,*
*Atop the Lean-To at Addis Gap,*
*Interrupted by a Disturbed Barn Owl\**

chuck-will-widow chuck-will-widow
*whip-poor-weel    whip-poor-weel*
chuck-will-widow chuck-will-widow
*whip-poor-weel    whip-poor-weel*
chuck-will-widow chuck-will-widow
*whip-poor-weel    whip-poor-weel*

## KSCHH! KSCHH! KSCHH! KSCHH! KSCHH! KSCHH! KSCHH!

chuck-will-widow chuck-will-widow
*whip-poor-weel    whip-poor-weel*
will                    will
*weel*                  *weel*
will                    will
*weel*                  *weel*
etc.                    etc.
*etc.*                  *etc.*

\* owleatoric theory bets on two more interruptions before the night is over

*La Source*

 

 

the Conasauga and the
Coosawattee
make the

Oostanaula


the Oostanaula and the
Etowah
make the
Coosa


flow
so

Napoleon Crossing the Rocky Mountains,
Sunrise on the Walls of Troy;

Tennessee Trouble in North Carolina,
Big Works of Tennessee;

Snail Trail,
Double Muscadine Hulls;


Catch Me If You Can!

*The Flower-Hunter in the Fields*

a flame azalea, mayapple, maple, thornapple
plantation

a white cloud in the eye
of a white horse


a field of bluets moving
below the black suit
of William Bartram

*bluets*, or 'Quaker Ladies,' or some say
'Innocence'


bluets and the blue of gentians and
Philadelphia blue laws!


high hills,

stone cold
sober


as October

*Iwauchuwa* in Japan; *Shortia galicifolia* in Transylvania and Oconee counties in the Southern Appalachians—the most legendary of our plants. Donald Culross Peattie is the custodian of the whole story. He has told it so beautifully in *Green Laurels* and in *The Great Smokies and the Blue Ridge* that it would be of no point for me to elaborate on his work. Suffice it, that a brief entry, dated December 8, 1788, in the journal of André Michaux was the beginning of a hundred years of investigation and search by Asa Gray, Charles Sprague Sargent, and other conspicuous American botanists. Michaux simply noted: ". . . I came across a new bush (*arbuste*) with notched leaves that was rampant on the mountainside not far from the river." He was at the headwaters of the Keowee (Kiwi, as he wrote it), below the confluence of the Horsepasture and Toxaway rivers as they have dropped from the ridge of the Balsam Mountains and levelled off above the present settlements of Tamassee and Jocassee in Oconee County, South Carolina. Today it is not difficult to find colonies of the plant under kalmia and rhododendron along the river.

There is another colony of plants further downriver these days, after the Keowee becomes the Savannah, there at Aiken/Augusta, where Thermonuclear Pale-Face works at the instruments of his destruction—or his salvation, it is probably one and the same. It seems questionable which species will outlast the other? The new flower-power dam put up by Duke Power tilts the balance in favor of man, but the America of Michaux and Bartram has been going down a rathole for a long time. It is interesting that William Bartram's grave is now unknown, though a two-day search in the Philadelphia area turned up for me the remains of father John. The stone is in the Quaker graveyard in Upper Darby, Pennsylvania, and the inscription reads: Approximate Grave of John Bartram . . .

If you despise a place long enough—this unruly continent, for instance— your own nature becomes somehow despicable. Man is a symbiot. There are places in the bald meadows of the Smokies where the bluets are windy clouds and the eye that reflects them is uncommonly lovely. Nowhere along the Appalachian Trail could I find a sacred grove, even in the Pennsylvania forest that Gifford Pinchot named for André and Francois Michaux. The trees were there, yet I could not find the citizens. Sacred for whom? to whom? The flawless boles of tulip poplars can be measured variously. Board feet by the hundred provide no wonder. I wondered whether the name of the god had not been drowned in the song of the wood thrush?

Paul McCartney's song "The Fool on the Hill" puts our deprivation as poignantly as I have heard it put. This magnificent composition, no less than the best of Schubert, Mahler, or Weill, atones for a lot in a deprived land-scape, as does a visit to Michaux's handsome little plant—before it is covered by venal water.

Edward Dahlberg writes in *The Sorrows of Priapus:* "The difference between a civilized and a detestable nation is in its votive fruits, spices, and animals. The Philistines, to appease the God of Israel, returned the stolen Ark with golden replicas of hemorrhoids. Aaron had an oracular Rod upon which almonds budded, and Perseus named the city of Mycene after a woody mushroom. Lucretius mentions the marjoram young suitors smeared on the door-posts of damsels. Solomon sang of the myrrh and sloes on the locks of the bridal door; Jesus ached for the alabaster of fragrant ointment the Pharisee denied him. 'Would to God that all the Lord's People were Prophets,' said Moses, who sighed for men whose souls smelled of frankincense and orchard fruits."

Dr. Charles Wilkins Short, the doctor-botanist of Kentucky, for whom Asa Gray named the plant, must have been such.

*An Aubade from Verlaine's Day*
(for Alfred Stieglitz)

the cloud in my head
wide to the edge of the world

the level cloud
that fills the Valley of the Little Tennessee
from Ridgepole to Rabun Bald

the laughter of
the Lord God Bird
Who pecks
berries
from the
dogwood

makes these two clouds
one, one eye
open

*The Deracination*

definition: *root,*
"a growing point,
an organ of absorption, an aereating organ,
a good reservoir, or
means of support"


*Vernonia glauca,* order *Compositae,*
"these tall perennials with
corymbose cymes of bright-purple heads of
tubular flowers
with conspicuous stigmas"


I do not know the Ironweed's root,
but I know it rules September

and where the flowers tower
in the wind there is a burr of
sound—empyrean . . . the mind
glows and the wind drifts . . .


epiphanies pull up
from roots—

*epiphytic,* making it up


out of the air

*The Rev. A. Rufus Morgan,*
*In His 93rd Year,*
*On Mount LeConte*

Rufus,

you reckon
there's anything
in Heaven

worth climbing
173 times?

*From Uncle Jake Carpenter's*
*Anthology of Death on Three-Mile Creek*

Loney Ollis
age 84
dide jun 10 1871

grates dere honter
wreked bee trees for hony
cild ratell snak by 100
cild dere by thousen


i nod him well

*To Carve in Wild Cherry*
*For John Jacob Niles*


30 dulcimers—
one long life


and what I said to the one of wild cherry was
bend a little, break later

where the bamma-gilly and the cow-cumber
flower forever
in a god's eye


out under the sky
out under the sky

*Epitaphs for Two Neighbors in Macon County*
*No Poet Could Forget*

## UNCLE IV OWENS

he done
what he could

when he got round
to it

## AUNT DORY OWENS

always
dahlies

always

*The Epitaph on Uncle Nick Grindstaff's Grave*
*On the Iron Mountain Above Shady Valley, Tennessee:*

## LIVED ALONE

## SUFFERED ALONE

## DIED ALONE

*The Whole Scene,*
*In a Two-Hundred-Year-Old*
*Demographic Nutshell*

                    a long row to hoe—
                    too wet to plough

*The publication of this book was supported*
*by grants from Douglas O. Chambers, Thomas L. Chatham, Noel Lee Dunn,*
*Frank Faulkner, Gordon & Copey Hanes, John Harbert, Barney Holland,*
*Thomas Lask, John Russell, Virginia Wilcox, and the*
*Lila Acheson Wallace Fund.*

*Composition & printing by Heritage Printers, Inc.*
*Garamond No. 3 has been used for the text, with added help*
*from Garamont, Hadriano, Ultra Bodoni, Cooper Black,*
*Brush, etc. as the occasions arose.*
*Design by Jonathan Greene*

*Of this edition, seventy-five copies*
*in slipcase have been signed and numbered*
*by the author.*